Stomachs

Written by Jo Windsor

CONTENTS

Stomachs	2
The Four-Stomached Cow	4
A Rabbit's Stomach	6
A Gorilla's Stomach	8
An Inside/Outside Stomach	10
A Frog's Stomach	12
A Stomach of Stones	14
Index	17

Stomachs

A stomach is like a stretchy pouch inside a body. It stores and softens food, getting it ready to be digested.

Some animals have one stomach; some animals have more than one stomach. Some animals even have stomachs that move outside the body!

Read on and you will find out some wonderful things about the stomachs of the animals in this book!

Glossary

Here are some words that you will need to know to help you read this book.

Cuds – digested food that comes back to the mouth from the stomach of an animal (such as a cow) to be chewed again.

Digested food – food that has been softened and broken down in the stomach.

Pellets – small balls of droppings.

Poisonous insect – an insect that can harm other animals with poison that it makes in its body.

Prey – an animal hunted or caught for food.

The Four-Stomached Cow

A cow has four stomachs. Each stomach has a special job to do.

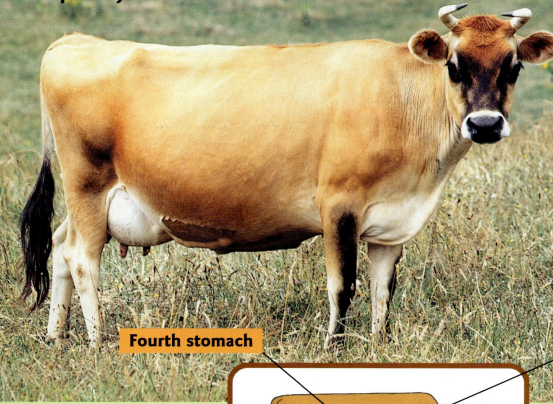

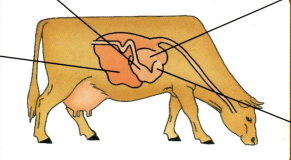

Fourth stomach

First stomach

Some Facts

A cow eats grass very quickly. The grass goes into the first stomach. This stomach mixes the grass until it is soft.

Then the grass goes into the second stomach. It is mixed again and made into small cuds. The cuds are brought back to the mouth. The cow will chew the cuds up to sixty times.

The cuds are swallowed and go on into the third stomach. Here they are mixed and softened more.

From this stomach, the food then goes to the fourth stomach. This is where the food is digested for energy.

A Rabbit's Stomach

It is hard for a rabbit to digest food, so it eats its food twice.

Stomach

Caecum

Some Facts

When a rabbit eats grass, or other food, it goes into the stomach. Then the food is pushed on into a pouch. This pouch is called a caecum.

When the food leaves the caecum, it goes on through the rabbit's body and comes out of the body as droppings. The droppings look like little pellets.

These droppings are then eaten by the rabbit. The food in the droppings needs to go through the rabbit's body twice to be digested for its energy.

A Gorilla's Stomach

A gorilla has one stomach . . . but it is very big.

Some Facts

Gorillas must eat a lot of food everyday. They eat the leaves, stems, roots and berries from plants. Sometimes, they will eat snails and insects such as ants.

After feeding, gorillas rest to let their food digest. The food is kept in the gorilla's huge stomach while it is digested. The digested food will make energy for the body.

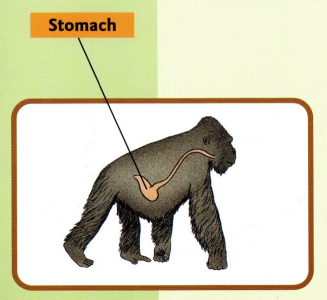

Stomach

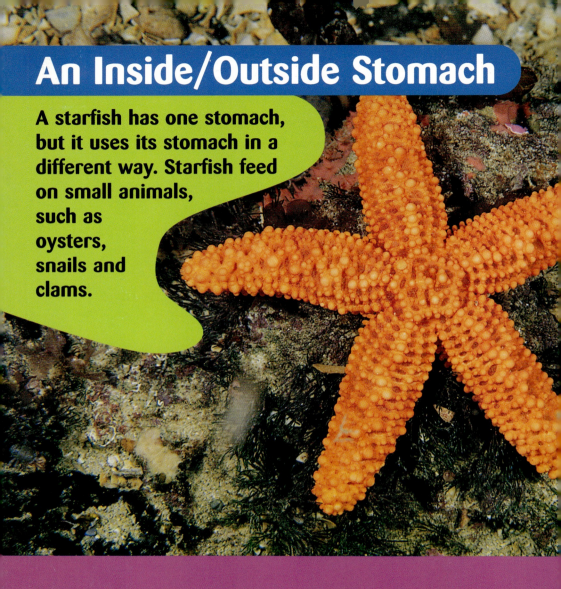

An Inside/Outside Stomach

A starfish has one stomach, but it uses its stomach in a different way. Starfish feed on small animals, such as oysters, snails and clams.

Some Facts

When the starfish eats, it slides its body over its prey. Its feet clamp on the prey and push against the shell. Soon the shell starts to come apart.

The starfish then puts its stomach out through its mouth into the shell. Now the starfish can digest the animal for its food.

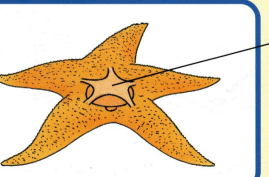

Stomach

A Frog's Stomach

A frog has one stomach but it can push its stomach outside its body.

Some Facts

Frogs eat mainly insects. Sometimes, a frog will swallow a poisonous insect. Then, the frog has to get rid of the insect quickly. The frog pushes its stomach out of its body. It uses its right front leg to scrape off the insect that is stuck to the stomach.

Stomach

A Stomach of Stones

Birds have no teeth.
They cannot chew their food.
When a bird eats, the food
goes through its beak
and down into its crop.

Some Facts

In the bird's crop, the food is made soft. The food then goes into the stomach to be stored, before it goes on into the gizzard.

The gizzard is a bag of muscles that grinds up the food into a pulp.

A bird eats little stones and stores them in its gizzard. These little stones help to grind up the food.

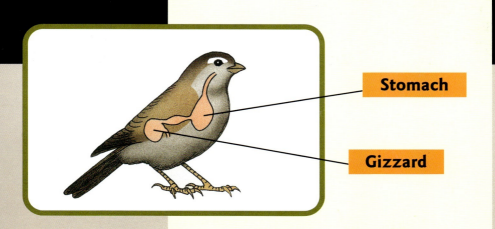

Stomachs

Has four stomachs to digit its food

Stomachs

Has one stomach – a very big one

Has one stomach that it can push out of its body

Has one stomach to digest its food

Index

bird stomach 14
cow stomach......................... 4
frog stomach 12
gorilla stomach 8
rabbit stomach...................... 6
starfish stomach 10

Has one stomach that it can push out of its body

Has one stomach and has stones in its gizzard to help grind up food

Explanation

Explanations explain how things work and why things happen.

How to write an explanation

Step One
- **Choose a topic.**
- **Make a list of the things you know about the topic.**

> **Topic:**
> Stomachs
>
> **What I know:**
>
> A stomach is inside the body.
>
> Some animals have more than one stomach.

- **Write down the things you need to find out.**

> **What I would like to find out:**
>
> Why do animals have different kinds of stomachs?
>
> How do their stomachs work?

Step Two
○ **Find out about the things you need to know. You can:**

> **Go to the library.**
>
> **Use the Internet.**
>
> **Ask an expert.**

○ **Make notes!**

Step Three
○ **Organize the information. Make some headings.**

Cow
Four stomachs

Food goes into each stomach.

Cuds are made in second stomach and go back to mouth to be chewed.

Rabbit
One stomach

Rabbits eat droppings to digest the food still in their droppings.

Step Four
○ **Use your notes to write your explanation!**

○ **You can use:**
diagrams, labels, illustrations, photographs, charts, tables and graphs.

Guide Notes

Title: Stomachs
Stage: Launching Fluency

Text Form: Informational Explanation
Approach: Guided Reading
Processes: Thinking Critically, Exploring Language, Processing Information
Written and Visual Focus: Explanation, Diagrams, Labels, Contents Page, Index, Glossary

THINKING CRITICALLY
(sample questions)
- What do you think this book is going to tell us?
- Focus the children's attention on the contents page. Ask: "What things are you going to find out about in this book?"
- Look at the index. Ask: "What are the things you want to find out about stomachs? What page would you turn to in the book?"
- Why do you think gorillas have to eat a lot of food each day?
- Why do you think the food is made soft in the bird's crop?

EXPLORING LANGUAGE

Terminology
Photograph credits, index, contents page, imprint information, ISBN number

Vocabulary
Clarify: muscles, pouch, poisonous, cuds, energy
Nouns: stomach, cow, frog, rabbit, starfish
Verbs: eat, chew, push
Singular/plural: stomach/stomachs, stone/stones, insect/insects

Print Conventions
Apostrophe – possessive (frog's stomach, rabbit's body, bird's crop)
Slash: (inside/outside stomach)
Parenthesis: (such as a cow)